DATA PROTECTION, PRIVACY AND PROPOSED LAW IN INDIA

Tracing the Previous Challenges and Transition to the Bill of 2021

DATA PROTECTION, PRIVACY AND PROPOSED LAW IN INDIA

Tracing the Previous Challenges and Transition to the Bill of 2021

Aana Sharma

ELIVA PRESS

ISBN: 978-99949-8-560-9

Cover Design: Eliva Press
Cover Image: Ingimage
Email: info@elivapress.com
Website: www.elivapress.com

This Eliva Press imprint is published by the registered company Eliva Press Global Ltd. part of Eliva Press S.R.L. Publishing Group

The registered company address is: Pope Hennessy Street Level 2, Hennessy Tower Port Louis, Mauritius
Eliva Press S.R.L. Publishing Group address is: Bulevardul Moscova 21, Chisinau, Moldova, Europe

DATA PROTECTION, PRIVACY AND PROPOSED LAW IN INDIA: Tracing the Previous Challenges and Transition to the Bill of 2021

Aana Sharma

Recommended Citation:

Aana Sharma, *DATA PROTECTION, PRIVACY AND PROPOSED LAW IN INDIA: Tracing the Previous Challenges and Transition to the Bill of 2021* II HPNLU. L. J. 55 (2021).

Table of Contents

I 3

Introduction 3

II 5

Concept of Privacy and Right to Privacy 5

III 9

Tracing the Development of Right to Privacy in India 9

IV 11

The *Modus Operandi* of Misuse of Data and the Need for Protection 11

V 15

Need for Data Protection Framework in India 15

VI 19

Conception of Supervisory Authorities and the European Data Protection Board under the GDPR 19

***How has the GDPR fared thus far?* 22**

***Independence of Supervisory Authorities* 22**

***The conception of DPAI* 24**

***Independence of DPAI* 26**

***Data Protection Board of India under the Digital Personal Data Protection Bill, 2022* 33**

VII 34

Conclusion 34

DATA PROTECTION, PRIVACY AND PROPOSED LAW IN INDIA: Tracing the Previous Challenges and Transition to the Bill of 2021

Aana Sharma

Aana Sharma*

*[**Abstract:** This paper attempts to critically analyze the draft bill of 2019. It further seeks to provide the critical analysis through drawing a comparison between the proposed statutory authority and the European Data Protection Board (hereinafter referred to as 'EDPB') under the General Data Protection Regulation (hereinafter referred to as 'GDPR') with that of Data Protection Authority of India (hereinafter referred to as 'DPAI') and consequently juxtaposing the idea of establishing DPAI with the other statutory authorities currently operating in India. The paper has also relied on the judicial pronouncements to clearly set out the view point of Indian Judiciary on clear demarcation of rights to privacy in India under its Constitutional framework. The new Bill of 2022 is only the vantage point of disrupting the right to privacy and the structural framework proposed therein comes with more limitations than discussed in this paper.]*

I

Introduction

Privacy to be secured through legislation and its justiciability as desired occurs with changing society. The individual as the bearer of rights mostly finds himself isolated from the group; the group which determined his rights in conservative terms, in the past.[1] Since, twentieth century, with his new found liberty the individual achieved the

* Post Graduate Student (LL.M.), National Law Institute University, Bhopal, India.

1 Dhikhu Parekh, *The Modern Conception of Right and its Marxist Critique*, 13(3-4) INDIA INT'L CENT. Q. VOL. THE RIGHT TO BE HUMAN 4 (1986) at 7-9.

best of self-assertion, but lost the group identity which safeguarded what was totally her/his private affair. The gregarious nature always drew him closer to the fanciful idea of getting noticed and their actions to be judged by the community as spectacular. This milieu gave birth to the inevitable platform of social and electronic media[2] so much so that the individual is even ready to pay for being read, commented, discussed and spoken about by people entirely unknown[3] to her/him. The rapid advancement in the digital economy worldwide in the past few decades has witnessed a new digital revolution. With the assumption of the established knowledge of the individual's desire to be part of the individuated society, this Paper tries a descriptive analysis to bring forth the main highlights of rights and duties of the individual and powers of regulation of the proposed statutory authority in Personal Data Protection Bill, 2019 (hereinafter referred to as the 'PDP Bill').[4]

This paper attempts to critically analyse the draft bill of 2019. It further seeks to provide the critical analysis through drawing a comparison between the proposed statutory authority and the European Data Protection Board (hereinafter referred to as 'EDPB') under the General Data Protection Regulation (hereinafter referred to as 'GDPR') with that of Data Protection Authority of India (hereinafter referred to as 'DPAI') and consequently juxtaposing the idea of establishing DPAI with the other statutory authorities currently operating in India. The paper has also relied on the judicial pronouncements to clearly set out the view point of Indian Judiciary on clear demarcation of rights to privacy in India under its Constitutional framework. The new Bill of 2022 is only the vantage point of disrupting the right to privacy and the structural framework proposed therein comes with more limitations than discussed in this paper.

---

2 The globalisation and advance technological revolution being the fuel to fulfil the desire of being noticed and getting a subscription to a group who may be identified as aficionados. The desirability and fulfilment of a specific purpose has also been one of the reasons why some technologies are lapped up by almost all human beings and some rejected.

3 Unknown socially, culturally, nationally and even linguistically.

4 Personal Data Protection bill, 2019 *available at*: https://prsindia.org/files/bills_acts/bills_parliament/2019/Personal%20Data%20Protection%20Bill,%202019.pdf.

II

Concept of Privacy and Right to Privacy

Much discourse by numerous scholars and philosophers has been around to understand the concept and ambit of privacy vis-a-vis right to privacy. Attempts have been made by such scholars to give an apt definition of the right to privacy. But in order to understand the contours or the concept of right to privacy as a whole, it becomes imperative to understand the individualistic, simple to sound yet complex term 'privacy'. The Merriam webster[5] dictionary defines privacy as: *'the quality or state of being apart from company or observation'.* This definition and many such other definitions given in other lexicons[6] have attempted to define privacy in a very simple layman-friendly terms. However, when the term 'privacy' is coupled with the expression 'right', its meaning can take a lot of varied forms and can change the perspective of how the expression 'right to privacy' is to be construed as a whole. That is to say, one may have a notion of privacy attached to a thing, person, or property but may not have a right of privacy associated with that thing, person or property. might seem very reasonable to a person as forming part of one's privacy, but it will certainly not give them the right to claim privacy over it. Alternatively, it may be the other way round as well. Also, at times, we might be oblivious about how to 'claim' our right to privacy and might even end up waiving it.[7]

Scholars and legal luminaries have claimed that it is difficult to define the concept of privacy. J.J Thomson argues that: '*the right to privacy is itself a cluster of rights, and that it is not a distinct cluster of rights but itself intersects with the cluster of rights which the right over the person consists in and also with the cluster of rights which*

---

5 *Privacy, available at:* https://www.merriam-webster.com/dictionary/privacy.

6 Oxford learner's dictionary defines privacy as: *'the state of being alone and not watched or interrupted by other people' available at:* https://www.oxfordlearnersdictionaries.com/definition/english/privacy.

7 J. Angelo Corlett, *The Nature and Value of the Moral Right to Privacy*, 16(4) PUBLIC AFFAIRS QUART 329 (2002).

owning property consists in'.[8] In other words, the right to privacy is not to be viewed as a basic right in itself, but rather as a 'derivative' right. It is derivative in the sense that it is derived from other fundamental rights such as the right to liberty, the right to life, and so on. This essentially means that right to privacy intersects and overlaps itself with other types of rights. For example, 'the right not to be looked at face' or 'the right not to be listened to' are a part of 'the right over the person'[9] and are similar to rights on property which a person has.[10] The idea of such rights being a part of privacy might sound crazy but as per the definition given by J.J Thomson, they technically fall in the domain of right to privacy. Thus, it can be said that there is no fixed boundary within which the right to privacy can be enclosed.

Brandeis in his seminal article defines right to privacy as: *'The right to privacy' is the right to be left alone.*[11] Similarly, Rachel L. Finn, David Wright and Michael Friedewald, in their paper titled as *'Seven Types of Privacy'*[12] stated:

'Privacy' is a key lens though which many new technologies, and most especially new surveillance technologies, are critiqued. However, 'privacy' has proved notoriously difficult to define. Serge Gutwirth says 'The notion of privacy remains out of the grasp of every academic chasing it. Even when it is cornered by such additional modifiers as 'our' privacy, it still finds a way to remain elusive.'[13] *Colin Bennett notes that 'attempts*

---

8 Judith Jarvis Thomson, *The Right to Privacy*, 4 PHILOSOPHY & PUBLIC AFFAIRS 31 (1975).

9 *Id.*, at 14.

10 Richard B. Parker, *A Definition of Privacy*, RUTGERS LAW REVIEW 281 (1974); author defines privacy as: *'The definition of privacy defended in this article is that privacy is control over when and by whom the various parts of us can be sensed by others. By 'sensed,' is meant simply seen, heard, touched, smelled, or tasted. By 'parts of us,' is meant the parts of our bodies, our voices, and the products of our bodies. 'Parts of us' also includes objects very closely associated with us. By 'closely associated' is meant primarily what is spatially associated. The objects which are 'parts of us' are objects we usually keep with us or locked up in a place accessible only to us.'*

11 S. Warren and L. Brandeis, *The Right to Privacy*, 4 HARV. L. R. 193-220 (1890).

12 R.L. Finn, D. Wright, & M. Friedeald, *Seven Types of Privacy* in EUROPEAN DATA PROTECTION: COMING OF AGE 3 (S. Gitwirth, *et.al.* (eds.) 2013).

13 *See,* Serge Gutwirth, PRIVACY AND THE INFORMATION AGE 30 (2002).

to define the concept of 'privacy' have generally not met with any success'.[14] *Legal scholars James Whitman and Daniel Solove have respectively described privacy as 'an unusually slippery concept'*[15]*, and 'a concept in disarray. Nobody can articulate what it means'*[16]*. Furthermore, Debbie Kaspar notes that 'scholars have a famously difficult time pinning down the meaning of such a widely used term [and] ... most introduce their work by citing this difficulty'.*[17] *Helen Nissenbaum has argued that privacy is best understood though a notion of 'contextual integrity', where it is not the sharing of information that is a problem, rather it is the sharing of information outside of socially agreed contextual boundaries.*[18]

Scholar Adam Moore wrote an article titled as 'Defining Privacy' wherein it was argued that if privacy exists in various fields, requiring varying degrees of protection, it would be incongruent to define it within the Constitutional framework as one overarching.[19] In the said article following it was argued by Adam Moore:

'Privacy has been defined in many ways over the last few hundred years.[20] *Warren and Brandeis, following Judge Thomas Cooley, called it 'the right to be let alone,'*[21] *Pound and Freund have defined privacy in terms of an extension personality or personhood.*[22] *Legal scholar William Prosser separated privacy cases into four distinct but related torts. 'Intrusion: Intruding (physically or otherwise) upon the solitude of another in a highly offensive manner. Private facts: Publicizing highly offensive private information about someone which is not of legitimate concern to the public. False light: Publicizing*

---

14 *See generally,* Colin J. Bennett, REGULATING PRIVACY: DATA PROTECTION AND PUBLIC POLICY IN EUROPE AND THE UNITED STATES (1992).

15 James Q. Whitman, *The Two Western Cultures of Privacy: Dignity v. Liberty*, 113 YALE LAW JOURNAL (2004).

16 Daniel Solve, *'I've Got Nothing to Hide' and Other Misunderstandings of Privacy*, 44 SAN DIEGO L. R. 758 (2007).

17 Debbie V.S. Kaspar, *The Evolution (or Devolution) of Privacy*, 20 SOCIOLOGICAL FORUM 72 (2005).

18 Helen Nissenbaum, PRIVACY IN CONTEXT: TECHNOLOGY, POLICY, AND THE INTEGRITY OF SOCIAL LIFE 75 (2009).

19 Adam Moore, *Defining Privacy*, 39(3) J. SOCIAL PHILOSOPHY 411 (2008).

20 *See generally*, Judith Wagner DeCew, IN PURSUIT OF PRIVACY: LAW, ETHICS, AND THE RISE OF TECHNOLOGY 1-4 (1997).

21 *See generally,* Thomas M. Cooley, COOLEY ON TORTS (1888).

22 Roscoe Pound, *Interests in Personality*, 28 HARV. L. R. 343 (1915); *See,* Paul A. Freund, *Privacy: One Concept Or Many?* 13 NOMOS: AM. SOC'Y POL. LEGAL PHIL. 182 (1971).

a highly offensive and false impression of another. Appropriation: Using another's name or likeness for some advantage without the other's consent.'[23]

Alan Westin has described privacy in terms of information control.[24] William Parent argues: *'[p]rivacy is the condition of not having undocumented personal knowledge about one possessed by others'.*[25] Julie Inness defined privacy as *'the state of possessing control over a realm of intimate decisions, which include decisions about intimate intimate information, and intimate actions.'*[26] Judith Wagner DeCew, on the other hand, had proposed that the *'realm of the private to be whatever types of information and activities are not, according to a reasonable person in normal circumstances, the legitimate concern of others.'*[27]

Similarly, on the question of the moral right to privacy, there are two polar theories, 'Privacy Respecting Theory' and 'Privacy Rejecting Theory'.[28] The former completely respects one's moral right to privacy and the latter rejects it. The privacy respecting theory views right to privacy as the fundamental to all other rights.[29] The privacy rejecting theory on the other hand view privacy as an obstacle to growth and harmony in society.[30] The moral right to privacy can be defined as a valid claim and/or interest[31] in being free to do what one wants to do.[32] In order to resolve the conflict between

---

23 Dean William Prosser, *Privacy*, 48 CALIFORNIA L. R. 383, 389 (1960) quoted in E. Alderman and C. Kennedy, THE RIGHT TO PRIVACY 155-56 (1997).

24 *See,* Alan F. Westin, PRIVACY AND FREEDOM 112 (1968); Adam D. Moore, INTELLECTUAL PROPERTY AND INFORMATION CONTROL 90 (2001, 2004).

25 W.A. Parent, *Privacy, Morality, and the Law*, 12 PHILOSOPHY AND PUBLIC AFFAIRS 269 (1983).

26 Julie Inness, PRIVACY, INTIMACY, AND ISOLATION 67 (1992).

27 *Supra* note 20.

28 *Supra* note 25.

29 *Supra* note 26.

30 C. Keith Boone, *Privacy and Community*, SOCIAL THEORY AND PRACTICE 9 (1983).

31 Stanley I. Benn, *The Protection and Limitation of Privacy*, 52 AUSTRALIAN L. J. 601 (1978).

'One must, however, exercise caution in referring to privacy as an interest. For to do so itself presupposes that it is something people would be better (or believe they would be better) for having, and that already amounts to an evaluative presupposition in its favour'.

32 *See* Eric Mack, *In Defense of the Jurisdiction Theory of Rights*, 4 THE JOURNAL OF ETHICS 71-98 (2000).

these two theories, J. Angelo Corlett proposed a middle path by devising a theory known as a 'Hybrid Theory of the Moral Right to privacy'. It is a hybrid of both the privacy respecting and rejecting theory as it acknowledges the opposing intuitions that lie behind both the theories. Author argues that this can serve as the foundation for a full-fledged theory of privacy, one that not only bridges ideological gaps in political, legal, and social theory, but also aids in understanding the crucial role that the idea of harm plays in a proper theory of the right to privacy.[33]

III

Tracing the Development of Right to Privacy in India

The entire discourse as to whether there exists a fundamental right to privacy in the Indian context, can be traced back to the catena of judgments of the Apex Court of India starting from *M.P. Sharma v. Satish Chandra*[34] to *K.S. Puttaswami* v. *Union of India,* where the Supreme Court of India has finally laid the matter to rest by recognizing right to privacy as a fundamental right granted under the article 21 of the Constitution of India. In *M.P Sharma* v. *Satish Chandra* and consequently in *Kharak Singh* v. *State of U.P.*[35], the Apex court held that right to privacy was not a 'guaranteed right' under Part III of the Constitution of India. The decisions in M.*P Sharma* as well as *Kharak Singh* were premised on an understanding of Part III as per the law laid down in *A.K. Gopalan* v. *State of Madras.*[36] *A.K. Gopalan* was specifically overruled in *Rustom Cavasjee. Cooper* v. *Union of India*[37] and thereafter further clarified to be so in *Maneka Gandhi* v. *Union of India.*[38] Thereafter, consistently for almost four and half decades, the Hon'ble Court has in a catena of judgments held that *A.K Gopalan* is bad

[33] *Supra* note 31.

[34] (1954) S.C.R. 1077.

[35] AIR 1963 S.C. 1295.

[36] (1950) S.C.R. 88.

[37] (1970) 1 SCC 248

[38] (1978) 1 SCC 248

law.[39] More importantly, once Gopalan was held to be bad law by an eleven-Judge Bench in *Rustom Cavasjee Cooper*, smaller Benches of the Apex Court have consistently and rightly held that the observations in *M.P. Sharma* and the majority judgment in *Kharak Singh* on the right to privacy were not good law.

A.K. Gopalan was overruled by *R.C. Cooper* in the following words:

'55. ... In our judgment, the assumption in A.K. Gopalan case that certain articles in the Constitution exclusively deal with specific matters and in determining whether there is infringement of the individual's guaranteed rights, the object and the form of the State action alone need be considered, and effect of the laws on fundamental rights of the individuals in general will be ignored cannot be accepted as correct.'[40]

In *Gobind* v. *State of M.P.*[41] Mathew, J. in unequivocal terms after noticing *Kharak Singh*, held that the right to privacy is implicit in the concept of individual autonomy and liberty. However, the Court categorically stated that it is not an absolute right and can be subjected to restrictions based on compelling public interest. The Court observed that the contours of the right will have to go through a process of case-by-case developments. It was observed by the Court:

'28. The right to privacy in any event will necessarily have to go through a process of case-by-case development. Therefore, even assuming that the right personal liberty, the right to move freely throughout the territory of India and the freedom of speech create an independent right of privacy as an emanation from which one can characterize as a fundamental right, we do not think that the right *is absolute.'*[42]

---

39 *See*, *I.R. Coelho* v. *State of T.N.*, (2007) 2 SCC 1, paras 30, 56, 57, 59, 61 & 172; *M. Nagaraj* v. *Union of India* (2006) 8 SCC 212, para 20; (2007) 1 SCC (L&S) 1013; *Selvi* v. *State of Karnataka* (2010) 7 SCC 263, paras 209, 225 : (2010) 3 SCC (Cri) 1; *Mohd. Arif* v. *Supreme Court of India* (2014) 9 SCC 737, para 26 : (2014) 5 SCC (Cri) 408.

40 AIR 1970 SC 564 para-55.

41 (1975) 2 SCC 148.

42 *Id.*, para-28.

The court in Gobind also took note of the decision of *Roe v. Wade*[43], where the litigant wanted to exercise the right to abortion and the Court recognised *'that a right of personal privacy or a guarantee of certain areas or zones of privacy, does exist under the Constitution'.* The Court in *Gobind* also clearly noticed that right to privacy contained multiple aspects[44], such as:

a. Spatial privacy;

b. Informational privacy;

c. Decisional autonomy; and,

d. Full development of personality;

Subsequently, many judgments of the Apex Court have relied on Gobind and decided that the right to privacy is a fundamental right guaranteed under the Indian Constitution. Finally, the nine judges' constitutional bench of the Apex Court in *K.S. Puttaswami* v. *Union of India* upheld the validity of right to privacy in the Indian Constitution and declared it as a fundamental right.

IV

The *Modus Operandi* of Misuse of Data and the Need for Protection

According to the IAMAI-Kantar ICUBE 2020 report, it has been estimated that the number of active internet users in India will increase to 900 million by 2025 from the present 622 million.[45] Every single activity being performed by us involves some kind of digital transaction. Metaphorically, it has been said that *'Personal data is the new*

---

43 410 US 113 (1973).

44 *Supra* note 41 at para 21-25.

45 Economic Diplomacy Division, *Internet usage in India to grow exponentially by 2025*, MINISTRY OF EXTERNAL AFFAIRS, GOVERNMENT OF INDIA (04 Jun., 2021) *available at*: https://indbiz.gov.in/internet-usage-in-india-to-grow-exponentially-by-2025/ (last visited 15 Jun., 2021).

oil of the internet.... '.[46] This 'oil' is mined using wells called 'cookies'. This 'oil' is then sold to 'refineries' to produce the 'fuel' that is needed to run the economic, marketing and corporate world. This oil can be anything- the number of times a person zooms in on the image a camera on a photojournalism website or the different kinds of shoes he searches on google images or even his desire for either sugar free or milk chocolates etc. Every tiny activity on the internet is pertinent to some industry or the other. A camera maker like Nikon will be looking for a customer who drools at the thought of a camera. An insurance company is looking for a customer who is worried about their blood sugar levels. Every activity of a person on the internet is refined by the websites that they visit and shipped off to industries that need that information to target their next customers. The same holds true *mutatis mutandis*, for other social media and e-commerce platforms, such as Youtube, Ajio as well. The problem of the said activity is that while invading the privacy of the individual it is used to exercise power over the individual without the knowledge of the individual that his liberty has been affected by corporate behemoths of twenty first century. In this sense the exercise of liberty becomes a façade as the choices before the individual is a posed choice.[47]

The business model of such e-commerce and social media platforms entirely operates on the personal data of its users. They are building vast databases of individuals preferences by constantly tracking their behavior and, in a way, indirectly affecting their decision-making ability.[48] These platforms disguise their corporatocratic

---

[46] M Kuneva, *Keynote Speech - Roundtable on Online Data Collection, Targeting and Profiling*, EUROPEAN COMMISSION (31 Mar., 2009) *available at*: https://ec.europa.eu/commission/presscorner/detail/en/SPEECH_09_156 (last visited 15 Jun., 2021).

[47] Eric J. Johnson, THE ELEMENTS OF CHOICE WHY THE WAY WE DECIDE MATTERS 2 (2022).

[48] Michael L. Rustad, Sanna Kulevska, *Reconceptualizing the right to be forgotten to enable transatlantic data flow*, 28 HARV. J. L. & TECH. 349 (2015); *See*, Tom Goodwin, *The Battle is for Customer Interface*, TECHCRUNCH, *available at:* https://techcrunch.com/2015/03/03/in-the-age-of-disintermediation-the-battle-is-all-for-the-customer-interface/> (last visited 15 Jun., 2021).

'profiling'[49] of consumers under the veil of user convenience. The European Union Regulation of 2016 on data privacy defines 'profiling' as any form of automated processing of personal data consisting of the use of personal data to evaluate certain personal aspects relating to a natural person, in particular to analyse or predict aspects concerning that natural person's performance at work, economic situation, health, personal preferences, interests, reliability, behaviour, location or movements. Almost every website on the internet with considerable traffic uses the aforementioned tool known as 'cookies'.[50] Cookies are a data monitoring software that collects user activity while on that platform including the part of the website, he/she spends the most time, any hyperlink they click on or on any picture that they zoom on. For instance, Amazon or Flipkart tracks the person's location and shopping preferences while on the website. Using this data any corporate entity can snipe its next consumer. For instance, a boy with meagre means who wants to learn photography, somewhere down the line, right now unable to purchase a professional camera. If he does divulge his interests over internet and this is also collated with data that how many types of professional cameras he searches for, frequently. It is often seen that over the next couple of weeks he will be bombarded with advertisements of how some other random boy from an impoverished background who purchased a camera went on a wildlife trek clicked a stunning picture of a lion, won the world's most prestigious photography awards and went on to make millions of dollars. Although impractical, the advertisement exaggerated the sentimental value of the camera and preys on consumers' emotions. This impairs the consumers' decision making ability who starts to relate to the advertisement and is now unsure whether to keep his saving or splurge them on a brand-new irrelevant piece of electronics. This affects the real exercise of liberty by the boy in this case. The very same dilemma was the subject matter dealt by the Supreme Court

---

49 Regulation No. (EU) 2016/679 of the European Parliament and of the Council of 27-4-2016 on the protection of natural persons with regard to the processing of personal data and on the free movement of such data, and repealing Directive No. 95/46/EC (General Data Protection Regulation).

50 *See*, Richie Koch, *Cookies, the GDPR, and the ePrivacy Directive*, GDPR.EU, *available at:* https://gdpr.eu/cookies/ (last visited 20 May, 2021).

of India in the landmark judgment of *K.S. Puttaswamy* v. *Union of India*[51] ('Puttaswamy') as well, which recognized the right to privacy as a fundamental right under article 21 of the Constitution of India. It was observed:[52]

'Uber', the world's largest taxi company, owns no vehicles. 'Facebook', the world's most popular media owner, creates no content. 'Alibaba', the most valuable retailer, has no inventory. And 'Airbnb', the world's largest accommodation provider, owns no real estate. Something interesting is happening.' 'Uber' knows our whereabouts and the places we frequent. 'Facebook' at the least, knows who we are friends with. 'Alibaba' knows our shopping habits. 'Airbnb' knows where we are travelling to. Social network providers, search engines, e-mail service providers, messaging applications are all further examples of non-State actors that have extensive knowledge of our movements, financial transactions, conversations — both personal and professional, health, mental state, interest, travel locations, fares and shopping habits. As we move towards becoming a digital economy and increase our reliance on internet-based services, we are creating deeper and deeper digital footprints — passively and actively.

Although the whole operation is shrouded by the wheel of two aspects- algorithms and plausible deniability-data mining and its subsequent profiling has had a significant impact on global events. For instance, the apple of this discord was Facebook when they had a class-action lawsuit filed against them over the previous decade. The lawsuit[53] led by senior attorneys of the US government was regarding the violation of the 1986 ECPA better known as the Wiretap Act. Facebook has been using like popups on independent websites to track the user's activity on that particular website. Consequently, it used that data to show tailor made acts to that person while scrolling on Facebook, causing the same impairment of decision-making ability as discussed above more frequent. This sort of data tracing and trading was strictly prohibited by

---

[51] (2017) 10 SCC 1.

[52] *Id.*, para – 589 at 619.

[53] *See, Lane et al v. Facebook, Inc. et al.*

the aforementioned ECPA Act, 1986. The same activity also had its implications in the US elections where Facebook was allegedly using advertisements and promoting right wing news outlets to change the decision of swing voters in favour of the republican party. Facebook used the two excuses, mentioned in the beginning of this paragraph, to deny its responsibility and shift the blame on technology. While the US government was quick to take action against the shrewd move not every government, especially in third world countries, is either prompt or concerned about the same.

V

Need for Data Protection Framework in India

India has always been in the need of a comprehensive legislative framework governing data protection. There has been no concrete law or framework for data protection in India thus far. One major law which comes to one's mind is the Information Technology Act, 2000[54] that governs and provides legal recognition to the transactions carried on in the electronic mode. However, the act is completely silent with respect to data protection and does little to protect individuals against the harms emanating from digital transactions in India. The only provision with respect to protecting data, that too only sensitive personal data, which one can see under the IT act is Section 43A[55] which holds a body corporate liable for compensation for any negligence in implementing and maintaining reasonable security practices and procedures while dealing with sensitive personal data or information (SPDI). Consequently, in order to regulate the transfer of personal data the Information Technology (Reasonable Security Practices and Procedures and Sensitive Personal Data or Information) Rules, 2011[56] ('SPDI

---

[54] Information Technology Act, 2000 (Act No. 21 of 2000).

[55] S.43A, Information Technology Act, 2000.

[56] Information Technology (Reasonable security practices and procedures and sensitive personal data or information) Rules, 2011.

Rules') were issued under section (2) of section 87[57] read with section 43-A of the IT Act on 13 April 2011. While the SPDI Rules can be said to be a novel attempt at data protection at the time of their introduction, however, the speed with which the digital economy has evolved has made it inevitable that some flaws have emerged in them over time. For instance, the definition of sensitive personal data[58] as given under the SPDI Rules is unduly narrow, leaving out several categories of personal data out from its protective remit.[59] Another major flaw is that its obligations do not apply to the government and may, on a strict reading of Section 43A of the IT Act be overridden by contract. In addition to these aforementioned flaws, the IT Act and SPDI Rules have also suffered from problems of implementation due to delays in appointments to the adjudicatory mechanisms created under the IT Act.[60]

Another very important reason which harps upon the need for a data protection framework is that with respect to India two observations can be made in today's date- India has one of the fastest growing FMCG market in the world[61] and the average Indian's purchasing power parity is miniscule compared to first world countries like the US and EU. Due to the growing size of FMCG market it is quite natural that this industry is looking for a much larger and streamlined consumer base to sell its products. However, as stated above and here the average Indian does not have enough money to inadvertently spend on consumer goods that he does not need. Corporations with the capacity to profile an individual using the data of their activity on the internet, their preferences or desires can effectively sway the citizens of an emotionally driven country like India to over purchase an unhelpful commodity or even purchase a needless commodity using social media marketing meant to invigorate their

---

57 S. 87, Information Technology Act, 2000.

58 Rule 3, SPDI Rules, 2011.

59 Graham Greenleaf, India, CONFUSION RAJ WITH OUTSOURCING IN ASIAN DATA PRIVACY LAWS: TRADE AND HUMAN RIGHTS PERSPECTIVES 415 (2017).

60 Sreenidhi Srinivasan and Namrata Mukherjee, *Building an effective data protection regime*, VIDHI CENTRE FOR LEGAL POLICY 18-19 (2017).

61 *See*, IBEF, *Indian FMCG Industry in India industry report, available at:* https://www.ibef.org/industry/fmcg.aspx (last visited 15 May, 2021).

sentiments. This can put pressure on individual financial holdings such as savings or provident funds which is integral to Indians.

In light of this, India is in the need of a comprehensive legislative framework governing data protection now more than ever. In order to address this long-felt need, the Ministry of Electronics and Information Technology (hereinafter referred to as 'MeitY') set up a nine-member committee of experts headed by Justice B.N. Srikrishna in July 2017, to study issues relating to data protection in India, and thereby to draft a comprehensive data protection bill. The need was further strengthened in the landmark judgment of *Justice K.S. Puttaswamy and Anr. v. Union of India and Ors.*[62] The apex court while recognizing the right to privacy as a fundamental right of the citizens of India, *inter alia,* emphasized that the Central Government should establish a robust data protection framework that balances the interests of individuals with the legitimate concerns of the state. It was observed by the apex court:

'Informational privacy is a facet of the right to privacy. The dangers to privacy in an age of information can originate not only from the state but from non-state actors as well. We commend to the Union Government the need to examine and put into place a robust regime for data protection. The creation of such a regime requires a careful and sensitive balance between individual interests and legitimate concerns of the state. The legitimate aims of the state would include for instance protecting national security, preventing and investigating crime, encouraging innovation and the spread of knowledge, and preventing the dissipation of social welfare benefits. These are matters of policy to be considered by the Union government while designing a carefully structured regime for the protection of the data. Since the Union government has informed the Court that it has constituted a Committee chaired by Hon'ble Shri Justice B N Srikrishna, former Judge of this Court, for that purpose, the matter shall be dealt

[62] *Supra* note 51.

with appropriately by the Union government having due regard to what has been set out in this judgment.'[63]

Emphasizing on the Puttaswamy judgment, the Srikrishna committee itself observed in its report that:

'The right to privacy has been recently recognised as a fundamental right emerging primarily from Article 21 of the Constitution, in Justice K.S. Puttaswamy (Retd.) v. Union of India. To make this right meaningful, it is the duty of the state to put in place a data protection framework which, while protecting citizens from dangers to informational privacy originating from state and non-state actors, serves the common good. It is this understanding of the state's duty that the Committee must work with while creating a data protection framework.'[64]

In the backdrop of the judgment[65] and the observation[66] of the Srikrishna Committee, on 27th July 2018, the Committee of Experts on Data Protection, under the Chairmanship of Justice BN Srikrishna, submitted its recommendations to the Ministry of Electronics and Information Technology, Government of India, in the form of a report: *A Free and Fair Digital Economy: Protecting Privacy, Empowering Indians* ('Srikrishna Report') along with a Draft Personal Data Protection Bill (hereinafter referred to as the 'Draft Bill')[67]. This draft was, thereafter, floated for public feedback till 10th October 2018[68]. After consulting with various stakeholders, the government set out to update the 2018 Draft Bill. Eventually, the revised version of the bill was

---

63 *Id.*, at para-328.

64 Committee of Experts under the Chairmanship of Justice B.N. Srikrishna, *A Free and Fair Digital Economy: Protecting Privacy, Empowering Indians*, MINISTRY OF ELECTRONICS AND INFORMATION TECHNOLOGY, *available at*: https://www.meity.gov.in/writereaddata/files/Data_Protection_Committee_Report-comp.pdf.

65 *Supra* note 51.

66 *Supra* note 64.

67 *Id.*

68 Ministry of Electronics and Information Technology, *Feedback on Draft Personal Data Protection Bill*, *available at*: https://meity.gov.in/content/feedback-draft-personal-data-protection-bill.

introduced in the Indian Parliament as the Personal Data Protection Bill, 2019 on December 11th, 2019[69].

VI

Conception of Supervisory Authorities and the European Data Protection Board under the GDPR

In 2018 a landmark regulation called the General Data Protection Regulation[70] (GDPR) was passed by the European Union (EU) to supersede and correct the flaws in its previous data protection act of 1995.[71] GDPR is a comprehensive regulation covering 99 provisions that deal with scope of application, legitimate grounds for processing, substantive obligations on data controllers and processors, rights of individuals to access, rectification, erasure and objections and establishment of appropriate enforcement machinery together with imposition of fines which extend up to 20,000,000 EUR, or in the case of an undertaking, up to 4% of the total worldwide annual turnover of the preceding financial year, whichever is higher.[72] GDPR comprehensively puts strict regulations on unconsent collection trading and use of personal data (defined as any information relating to an identified or identifiable natural person). GDPR also meticulously increased the ambit of personal data to cover all information that can be used to directly or indirectly identify individuals such as IP address, cookie IDs, biometrics, CCTVs, call recordings etc.,

---

69 *Supra* note 4.

70 Regulation (EU) 2016/679 (General Data Protection Regulation).

71 EU Data Protection Directive 95/46/EC.

72 *See*, GDPR article 83(5).

The European Union's GDPR, replaced the erstwhile1995 EU Data Protection Directive (DPD95)[73], and came into effect on May 25th, 2018.[74] It aims to harmonize the data protection regulations across the European Union by providing a one uniform data protection law. It aimed at avoiding fragmentation by having only one uniform law at place instead of having 28 data protection law for each member state. GDPR provides a framework of accountability for businesses processing personal data in the EU.[75]

EU was the first to adopt a specific regulation for the protection of data. Since then, almost 67 out of 120 countries outside Europe have largely adopted the European Union's (EU) General Data Protection Regulation[76] framework. Governments around the world have found it safe to adopt GDPR as it is updated to reflect the current digital age.[77] The Indian Personal Data Protection Bill 2019 is modelled after the GDPR.[78] The draft bill and the report, however, differ significantly in regulatory aspects from the EU GDPR's radical dispersal of decision-making responsibility.[79] In many aspects,

---

73 EU Data Protection Directive 1995 (Directive 95/46/EC of the European Parliament and of the Council of 24 October 1995 on the protection of individuals with regard to the processing of personal data and on the free movement of such data).

74 GDPR article 99(2): 'It shall apply from 25 May 2018.'

75 *See*, Lothar Determan, *GDPR Ante Portas: Compliance Priorities for the Impending EU Data Protection Regulation*, 2 PLI CURRENT: THE JOURNAL OF PLI PRESS (2018); *see also*, *Less Than 20 Weeks to the European Union GDPR-What to Do Now?* PRIVACY & SECURITY LAW REPORT (BNA) (2018) *available at:* https://www.bloomberglaw.com/document/X7GK4540000000?bc=W1 siQ210YXRpb24gUmVzdW.

76 Regulation (EU) 2016/679 of the European Parliament and of the Council of 27 April 2016 on the protection of natural persons with regard to the processing of personal data and on the free movement of such data, and repealing Directive 95/46/EC (General Data Protection Regulation), OJ 2016 L 119/1, *available at* http://ec.europa.eu/justice/data-protection/reform/files/regulation_oj_en.pdf.

77 Graham Greenleaf, *The Influence of European Data Privacy Standards outside Europe: Implications for Globalisation of Convention*, 20(2) INTERNATIONAL DATA PRIVACY LAW (2012).

78 Ram Govind Singh and Sushmita Ruj, *A Technical Look At The Indian Personal Data Protection Bill*, Indian Statistical Institute Kolkata, India (2020) *available at:* https://arxiv.org/pdf/2005.13812.pdf.

79 Graham Greenleaf, *GDPR-Lite and Requiring Strengthening – Submission on the Draft Personal Data Protection Bill to the Ministry of Electronics and Information Technology (India)* (2018) *available at* SSRN: https://ssrn.com/abstract=3252286 or http://dx.doi.org/10.2139/ssrn.3252286.

the Indian approach is more prescriptive in nature[80] (possibly closer to the 1995 EU Directive in this regard), and it does this by effectively delegating legislative duty to the DPAI (or, in some situations, the government). The primary reason for adopting the EU model in the Indian regulatory context is due to the rights-based approach which is being adopted in the GDPR as well. The relevance of EU's right based approach was highlighted in Justice Srikrishna Committee's report and was also reiterated in Puttuswamy judgment as well. This indicates that the Indian data protection framework highly resonates with that of GDPR.[81]

The important pillars which the framers had at back of their mind while framing GDPR were accountability, harmonization, and consistency of the GDPR pan-Europe. This accountability is being looked after by the Supervisory Authorities[82] (hereinafter referred to as 'SA or SAs') which act as the regulatory enforcement arms.[83] Each member state has its own supervisory authority and work independently[84] in their own spheres. These supervisory authorities enforce and advise on the data protection rules. Article 51[85] provides each member state to provide for one or more independent public authority (supervisory authority) to monitor the application of the regulation. Thus, member states are free to establish more than one supervisory authority.[86] Along with the SAs, GDPR also provides for a lead supervisory authority[87] which has been set for looking after cross-border data related issues and to ensure efficient investigation and consistent interpretation of its enforcement procedures across the EU.

---

80 *Id.*

81 Deva Prasad M and Suchithra Menon C, *The Personal Data Protection Bill, 2018: India's regulatory journey towards a comprehensive data protection law*, INTERNATIONAL JOURNAL OF LAW AND INFORMATION TECHNOLOGY 1 (2020).

82 GDPR article 4(21) defines data protection 'supervisory authority' as: '*an independent public authority that is established by a member state pursuant to Article 51*'. This definition reinforces the independence of data protection supervisory authorities.

83 Sanjay Sharma, DATA PRIVACY AND GDPR HANDBOOK 258 (2020).

84 *Id.*, para-19 at 259.

85 GDPR article 51.

86 *See* GDPR Recital 117.

87 GDPR article 56.

GDPR has also envisaged the idea of setting up of a board known as the European Data Protection Board[88] (hereinafter referred to as the 'the EDPB'). The advent of EDPB has replaced the working party on the protection of individuals with regard to the processing of personal data that was established by Directive 95/46/EC[89].The Board consists of the head of one supervisory authority of each member state and of the European Data Protection Supervisor, or their respective representatives.[90] The EDPB acts an independent body of the union. The board, thus, acts independently in performing its tasks.[91]

How has the GDPR fared thus far?

In a report published by the DIGITALEUROPE - *Two years of GDPR: A report from the digital industry*[92], several key elements were highlighted to improve GDPR. It has been observed in the report that strengthening the consistency and more coordinated implementation amongst member states is needed to effectively harmonise the law. The report also stresses on GDPR to be updated and keep abreast with the modern-day technological developments.

Independence of Supervisory Authorities

The important feature of EU's GDPR is that it ensures complete independence of the working of the Supervisory authorities.[93] Each SA has been granted an 'independent status.'[94] GDPR provides for each member state to provide for one or more independent public authorities to be responsible for monitoring the application of the GDPR so as to protect the fundamental rights of natural persons in relation to processing and to

---

88 GDPR article 68(1).

89 Directive 95/46/EC

90 GDPR article 68(3).

91 GDPR recital 139.

92 DIGITALEUROPE - Two years of GDPR: A report from the digital industry (2020).

93 GDPR recitals 121, 153 and articles 4, 51, and 52.

94 GDPR chapter VI.

facilitate the free flow of personal data within the EU.[95] In order to ensure independence in the working of SAs and commission, GDPR warrants the SAs to cooperate with each other and with the EU Commission in accordance with Chapter VII.[96] GDPR further ensures that each supervisory authority must act with complete independence in performing its tasks and exercising its powers in accordance with the GDPR.[97] Article 52(2) gives the freedom to the member or members of each data supervisory authority must, in the performance of their tasks and exercise of their powers in accordance with the GDPR, to remain free from external influence, whether direct or indirect, and neither seek nor take instructions from anybody.[98] This provision makes sure that the SAs remain independent in their functioning.

Article 52(4) provides each member state to ensure that each data protection supervisory authority is provided with the human, technical, and financial resources, premises, and infrastructure necessary for the effective performance of its tasks and the exercise of its powers, including those to be carried out in the context of mutual assistance, cooperation, and participation in the EDP.[99] Similarly, article 52(5) provides that each member state must ensure that each supervisory authority chooses and has its own staff, which must be subject to the exclusive direction of the member or members of the data protection supervisory authority concerned.[100] Another important article that ensures free functioning of SAs is article 52(6). It provides that each member state must ensure that each supervisory authority is subject to financial control that does not affect its independence and that it has separate, public annual budgets, which may be part of the overall state or national budget.[101]

95 GDPR article 51(1).

96 GDPR article 51(2).

97 GDPR article 52(1).

98 GDPR article 52(2).

99 GDPR article 52(4).

100 GDPR article 52(5).

101 GDPR article 52(6).

The conception of DPAI

Thinking on the same lines as that of GDPR, the Srikrishna Committee has envisaged the idea of setting up of an authority which shall be known as data protection authority of India i.e DPAI. There are considerable differences between the SAs and DPAI, which are being dealt with in the following paragraphs. However, what remains to be seen is how effective can such an authority turn out to be in protecting the privacy and upholding the rights of the individuals in the times to come. The past experience of India with respect to such statutory bodies has not been remarkable in fulfilling the aims for which such statutory body were set up for. Thus, drawing evidence from the problems faced in the past in the effective functioning of such statutory bodies, lessons should be learnt which can help save the legislature from committing the same mistake again and instead come up with some innovative and novel idea for effective regulation.

The DPAI shall serve as a regulatory and enforcement body. The DPAI has been vested with certain powers and functions to protect the interests of individuals, to prevent misuse of data by data-fiduciaries and to ensure effective functioning of the act. The concept of DPAI has been borrowed by the committee from the EU GDPR's European Data Protection Board and Supervisory Authorities.[102] Section 41[103] of the Personal Data Protection Bill, 2019 provides for establishing an authority to be known as Data Protection Authority of India (DPAI). Section 42[104] lays down the composition and qualifications for appointment of Members in DPAI. The authority shall consist of a Chairperson and not more than six whole-time Members.[105] The DPAI has been vested with certain wide powers[106] viz. investigative powers, corrective powers, power of search and seizure, authorization and advisory powers etc., and functions as well.

---

[102] Amba Kak, *The Emergence of the Personal Data Protection Bill, 2018 A Critique*, 53(38) EPW 12 (2018).

[103] S.41, The Personal Data Protection Bill, 2019 (Bill No. 373 of 2019).

[104] S.42, The Personal Data Protection Bill, 2019 (Bill No. 373 of 2019).

[105] *Id.*, section 42(1).

[106] *Id.* Ss. 49, 51, 52, 53 and 55.

The basic difference between DPAI and SAs is that under the GDPR, member states are free to establish one or more supervisory authorities. However, the PDPB provides for establishing only one central Data Protection Authority. The powers of SAs under GDPR and DPAI under PDPB are substantially similar, however, the DPAI has not been given an explicit power to order rectification or erasure of personal. The powers of DPAI are not absolute. This is evident from the scheme of the bill as the bill envisages the setting up of an Appellate Tribunal.[107] Thus, any person aggrieved by the decision of the DPAI may prefer an appeal to the Appellate Tribunal within a period of thirty days.[108] Further, an appeal can lie to the Supreme Court[109] against any order of the Appellate Tribunal, not being an interlocutory order, on any substantial question of law.

A rapid growth of advancement in the number of users of data[110], requires large regulatory capacity to regulate such data. However, as per World's bank *Ranking of Regulatory Quality Across Countries, 2018,*[111] India ranks way below those other countries which already have data protection laws in place such as UK, France and Germany. Given India's low regulatory capacity[112] and broad supervisory mandate of DPA, it is likely possible that the functioning of DPAI can be severely constrained and it will not be able to effectively execute the bill. DPAI may even struggle to develop internal capacity due to its cross-sectoral mandate. This can result in either under regulation or overregulation and will eventually defeat the intent of the bill.[113] At the same time, there is a high possibility that due to this low regulatory capacity DPAI

---

107 *Id.* S. 67.

108 *Id.* S. 72(1).

109 *Id.* S. 75(1).

110 UNCTAD, *Technology and Innovation Report 2018: Harnessing Frontier Technologies for Sustainable Development* (2018) *available at*: https://unctad.org/system/files/official-document/tir2018_en.pdf.

111 *See,* Ranking of Regulatory Quality Across Countries, 2018, World Governance Indicators, World Bank, *available at:* https://info.worldbank.org/governance/wgi/

112 *Id.*

113 Anirudh Burman, *Will India's Proposed Data Protection Law Protect Privacy and Promote Growth?*, CARNEGIE INDIA WORKING PAPER (2020) *available at*: https://carnegieendowment.org/files/Burman_Data_Privacy.pdf.

might enact a wide number of rules and regulations in order to mimic the appearance of effective regulation without taking into account the outcomes.[114] This phenomenon is known as 'isomorphic mimicry': *a 'combination of capability failure while maintaining at least the appearance and often the legitimacy and benefits of capability as 'successful failure.'*[115]

Independence of DPAI

One of the central pillars to ensure the effective operation of the data protection rules is the conception of DPAI. This authority is important for organizations to deal with not only in terms of normal processes but also in cases of problem issues or even contentious matters such as data breaches and complaints. Thus, it is important that DPAI must be conceived properly. This can be achieved when DPAI is given independence in performing its tasks or exercising its powers. The most apparent deficiency in the bill is the lack of independence of DPA from the government.[116] For instance, it is the complete discretion of the central govt. to appoint adjudication officers. Similarly, the power to give directions to regulators on 'matters of policy' also solely rests with the central government.

The problems which can crop up in future with the setting up of DPAI are:

1. **Pendency or backlog of cases -** The feature of pending cases in not a new factor in India, be it the courts or the commissions currently operating in India. One such commission is the National Human Rights Commission (hereinafter referred to as 'NHRC') that work for the protection and promotion of human rights in India. The NHRC was established under the Protection of Human

[114] *Supra* note 81.

[115] Matt Andrews, Lant Pritchett, and Michael Woolcock, LOOKING LIKE A STATE: THE SEDUCTION OF ISOMORPHIC MIMICRY (2017).

[116] *Supra* note 102.

Rights Act, 1993.[117] As per NHRC's twenty-fifth Annual Report (2017-18)[118] the total number of cases registered and disposed by the NHRC in the year 2017-2018 are 79,612 and 86,187, respectively. This figure of 86,187 cases also included cases of previous years as well. The total number of cases pending as on March 31st, 2018 are 25,775[119]. Out of this figure of 25,775, 2212 are the cases awaiting preliminary consideration and 23,563 are the pendency of cases where reports have either been received or awaited from the authorities. The reason for such pendency is best known to the authorities. This figure in itself speaks of the fact that there is some lacking on the part of the authorities which leads to such backlog. The reasons can be procedural or administrative anomalies, lackadaisical attitude of the officers etc.

Similarly, the total number of cases pending for compliance where NHRC recommended monetary relief are 606[120]. The amount associated with these cases is a humongous figure of seventeen crore two lakh five thousand (170205000). This indicates that fund allocation or cash crunch is also one of the factors affecting pendency of cases. As per NCW's Annual Report (2018-19) a total of 19,279 complaints/cases were registered. The detail of the number of cases pending and disposed of by the commission is not disclosed in the report.

The National Commission for women (NCW) is another such statutory body which was established in January 1992 under the National Commission for Women Act, 1990[121] to safeguard and protect the constitutional rights of women and provide adequate remedies to resolve the grievances of women. Similarly, National Green Tribunal[122] (NGT) is another statutory body that has been established on under the

---

[117] Protection of Human Rights Act, 1993 (No. 10 of 1994).

[118] National Human Rights Commission, ANNUAL REPORT (2017-18) *available at*: https://nhrc.nic.in/sites/default/files/NHRC_AR_EN_2017-2018.pdf.

[119] *Id.* Annexure 3.

[120] *Id.* Annexure 4.

[121] National Commission for Women Act, 1990 (No. 20 of 1990).

[122] National Green Tribunal Act, 2010 (No. 19 of 2010).

National Green Tribunal Act, 2010. It is a specialized body which deals with the expeditious disposal of cases related to environmental matters and works for the conservation of forests and other natural resources. The data regarding *Grand total of institution, disposal and pendency of the cases of ngt principal bench and all zonal benches from the date of its inception till 30.09.2021,*[123] from its website shows that 35963 cases have been instituted thus far out of which 33619 cases have been disposed off and 2344 cases are still pending.

The Annual Report 2019[124] of National Legal Services Authority (NALSA) claims that there has been a timely disposal of applications and appeals.

Drawing analysis from the data of commissions mentioned above, there is a high possibility that we might get to face the same issue with DPAI as well. Since DPAI is also of the nature of a statutory body. Getting to see such a result in case of DPAI will just add on to the existing pile of pending cases just like the other statutory bodies. Moreover, the bill also provides a mechanism of appeal from authority to the tribunal and then to the supreme court. The mechanism of appeal will elongate the process and will act as a barrier in proper and effective delivery of Justice. This eventually will prove to be a sorry state of affairs for the government once again.

2. **Appointment of officials and Vacancies**- The appointment of officials on various posts is another factor which can hamper the efficiency and credibility of DPAI. It has been seen that mostly retired governmental officials are appointed to such posts who neither have knowledge nor experience in the field of operation of the Commission. They function in a bureaucratic manner which eventually tend to affect the overall functioning of these commissions.[125] This is

---

[123] National Green Tribunal, *Grand Total Of Institution, Disposal And Pendency Of The Cases Of Ngt Principal Bench And All Zonal Benches From The Date Of Its Inception Till* (2022) *available at:* https://greentribunal.gov.in/.

[124] National Legal Services Authority, ANNUAL REPORT (2019), *available at:* https://nalsa.gov.in/library/annual-reports/annual-report-2019.

[125] Mandeep Tiwana, *Needed: More Effective Human Rights Commissions in India*, 11 CHRI NEWSLETTER 4 (2004) *available at*: https://www.humanrightsinitiative.org/publications/nl/articles/india/needed_more_effective_hr_comm_india.pdf

reflected in the overall outcome in terms of pending of cases of such commissions.

Another important flaw in such appointments is the pattern of unfulfilled vacancies which can be observed especially in respect of NHRC[126]. Most of these commissions function with less than the prescribed limit of members which in turn affects the ability of such commissions to deal with the large chunks of complaint. This eventually leads to huge backlog of cases. In *Dilip K. Basu* v. *State of West Bengal*[127] the court elaborated in great detail on the matter pertaining to the non-filling of vacancies in State Human Rights Commissions and also took note of the bureaucratic indifference and political pressure in the appointment of such vacancies. The court observed:

'...the very purpose of setting up of the State Human Rights Commission gets defeated if vacancies that occur from time to time are not promptly filled up and the Commission kept functional at all times. There is hardly any explanation much less a cogent one for the failure of the State to take immediate steps for filling up of the vacancies wherever they have occurred. The inaction or bureaucratic indifference or even the lack of political will cannot frustrate the laudable object underlying the parliamentary legislation...'.[128]

The judgment and observation of the court in *DK Basu* highlights the problem of appointment of bureaucratic officials and the unfilled vacancies plaguing the working of the commissions. Speaking on the same lines, the same problem as discussed above can be get to be seen in the functioning of DPAI as well. In order to overcome these problems, it becomes imperative that government should hire independent and competent staff members having adequate experience to handle the cases.[129]

3. **Resource allocation**- The independence of the DPAI is an important critical factor which can ensure its smooth functioning. One another way of ensuring

---

126 *Supra* note at 118.

127 (2015) 8 SCC 744.

128 *Id.*, para 28 at 768.

129 *Supra* note at 118.

this independence can be via providing adequate funds to it. For instance, DPAI should have a separate, public annual budget, which may be part of the overall state or national budget.

When the issues related to inadequacy of funding can arise in a developed union such as EU (reports of EU on budget allocation), then there is a high possibility of such problem to arise in the Indian context.

4. **Transparency and Accountability**- Transparency marks an important feature for the effective functioning of any authority. It helps in building trust among users. This in turn will ensure the independence of the DPAI. The bill imposes responsibility on the data fiduciary to maintain transparency.[130] However, the bill is silent about ensuring the transparency of the data protection authority of India. Disclosure of list of third parties with whom the govt. wishes to share data along with reasons of collecting data can be one way of ensuring transparency.[131]

Transparency is also essential to be maintained during the data breach[132]. Any issue related to data breach is to be reported to the DPAI.[133] The problem lies in maintaining the transparency when data breach is reported to the authority because if an external entity reports about breach to the authority, it would directly come under the radar of the authority. However, it would become difficult to ensure transparency when the data breach is reported internally as it would entirely depend on the honesty of data fiduciary. There are chances that data fiduciary might not report such data breach to the authority. This eventually will put a question mark on the transparency. Legally, the data authority can impose a penalty on the data fiduciary if such an event occurs, however, no technical solution exists to curb the same.[134]

---

[130] PDP Bill, 2019 section 23 states: 'the data fiduciary shall take reasonable step to maintain transparency...'.

[131] *Supra* note 64.

[132] In the framework data breach is stated as: 'any unauthorised, accidental disclosure, acquisition, sharing, use, alteration, destruction,...that compromise confidentiality, integrity or availability of personal data to data principal'.

[133] S. 25, PDP Bill, 2019.

[134] *Supra note* 64.

5. **Interference by the Central Government**- The scheme of the PDPB gives power to the central government to issue directions to the DPAI from time to time.[135] The bill provides that the decision of the central government shall be final, irrespective of whether a question involved is one of policy or not.[136] This provision gives ample power to the government to interfere in the functioning of DPAI. The central government also has been given wide powers to make rules and regulations.[137] Any personal data can be requested by the government for the purpose of state functioning, during an emergency, for state security, for the prevention, detection, investigation, or prosecution of any crime, or for any other law violation.[138] Disclosing data related to cross-border transfer, the pattern of security standard being followed by data fiduciary, the methodology of data collection method can be some other ways of ensuring transparency.[139] The bill does not provide any adequate checks and balances on the vast supervisory powers of the govt.

Furthermore, the bill also allows the government to exempt its agencies from complying with the provisions of the act.[140] This indirectly could provide a new source of power for national security agencies to conduct surveillance and, ironically, could dilute privacy instead of protecting it.[141] At the same time, bill also grants the govt. to frame rules and guidelines regarding 'such procedure, safeguards and oversight mechanism to be followed by the agency.'[142] This shows that the bill intends on strengthening the state without adequately protecting privacy.

---

[135] S.86(1), PDP Bill, 2019.

[136] *Id.* S. 86(3).

[137] *Id.* Ss. 93 & 94.

[138] *Id.* S. 12.

[139] *Supra* note 64.

[140] S.35, PDP Bill, 2019.

[141] *Supra* note 113.

[142] S.35, PDP Bill, 2019.

6. **Amount of penalty which can be imposed-** The Personal data protection act, 2019 has envisaged a GDPR-style penalty system.[143] For failing to notify data breaches to the Data Protection Authority, or failing to follow the Act's requirements, data controllers can be fined up to five crore rupees or 2% of global turnover.[144] Similarly, data controllers can be fined fifteen crore rupees or four per cent of global turnover[145] for failing to provide data subjects with notices indicating the existence of a legitimate basis for processing; performing unlawful cross-border data transfers; or processing children's data in contravention of Chapter IV of the act.[146]

A report produced by DLA Piper's cybersecurity and data protection team *DLA Piper GDPR fines and data breach survey: January 2021,*[147] a total of EUR272.5 million (about USD332.4 million / GBP245.3 million) of fines have been imposed for a wide range of infringements since the application of GDPR on 25 May 2018. Among all the member states, Italy topped of having imposed the maximum number of fines. It imposed fines of more than EUR69.3 million. The biggest GDPR fine thus far has been imposed on amazon. It was worth €746 million.[148]

Going by this data, in the Indian context also higher fines can be imposed by the DPAI to ensure a deterrent effect. This is turn will create a fear amongst data fiduciaries before breaching any data of the data principals and will in turn protect the privacy of the users.

7. **Flawed structural design-** The proposed structure of DPA in the framework lacks certain elements which can impact its functioning and transparency. For

---

143 Lothar Determann & Chetan Gupta, *India's Personal Data Protection Act, 2018: Comparison with the General Data Protection Regulation and the California Consumer Privacy Act of 2018*, 37 BERKELEY J. INT'L L. 481 (2019).

144 S. 57(1), PDP Bill, 2019.

145 *Id.* S. 57(2).

146 *Id.* S. 16.

147 DLA Piper GDPR fines and data breach survey (2021) *available at:* at www.dlapiper.com.

148 *20 Biggest GDPR Fines of 2019, 2020, and 2021 (So Far) available at:* https://www.tessian.com/blog/biggest-gdpr-fines-2020/.

instance, there are no independent members being added in DPA.[149] Independent members are essential to be added for ensuring transparency and effective functioning of any regulatory authority and especially for authorities which are of the nature of DPA. Independent members help in providing independent inputs and in a way instills trust and confidence in the users. At the same time, the bill does not provide any provision for the consultative process to be followed by the government and the DPA while promulgating codes of practice.[150] This shows that there are no adequate checks and balances on the regulating framing powers of the government and DPAI. Such a flawed structural design can affect the protection of privacy for which the framework has been set up.

In order to overcome the abovementioned structural irregularities and problems, the bill should be modified to ensure that the govt. and DPAI follow detailed and adopt best practices for regulation-making. Cost-benefit analysis of the data protection can help in designing a more pragmatic and precise regulatory framework suitable to needs of the Indian economy.[151]

Data Protection Board of India under the Digital Personal Data Protection Bill, 2022

The bill by virtue of its Chapter V (Compliance Framework) envisages the set-up of a board to be called as the data protection board of India (hereinafter to be called as 'the board'). It can be clearly ascertained from a fair reading of section 19[152] that a considerable amount of power has been given to the central government which can pull the strings of the board as and when it desires. This is because along with the task of establishment of the board, central government has also been bestowed with the power

[149] S.42, PDP Bill, 2019.

[150] S. 50(4), PDP Bill, 2019.

[151] *Supra* note 113.

[152] S.19, Digital Personal Data Protection Board, 2022.

of selection of the members and composition of the board. The process of selection, tenure, terms and conditions of appointment and service of the members along with the management of affairs of the board has also been given to the central government. Even the powers given to the board are merely on the paper as there is intervention of the central government in assigning functions to the board which the government may so desire.[153]

These wide-ranging powers provided to the central government hints towards the reduced independence of the board and against the spirit of section 21[154] of the draft bill itself. Under the 2019 bill, the data protection authority was a statutory authority whereas this newly constituted board under the newly drafted bill is a central government set up board. This hinges upon the unbridled power given to the government, which is prone to be misused. The central government holds power to grant exemptions to its agencies from adhering to the provisions of the draft law under the garb of 'national and public interest'. This is also prone to being misused because of the vagueness of the expression 'national and public interest'.[155] Here, individual interest has the possibility of getting sidelined because of the national interest.

VII

Conclusion

The concept of privacy has gained prominence only in the recent times especially with the advent of internet because, out of ignorance, the individuals have allowed their privacy to be infringed by corporate behemoths. The exercise of power over the individual by few, continues through neo-capitalism without the knowledge of the so-

153 *Id.* S. 20.

154 *Id.*.

155 Lynn Pasquerella & Alfred G. Killilea (2005) *The Ethics of Lying in the Public Interest: Reflections on the 'Just Lie', Public Integrity*, Taylor & Francis Online, 7:3, 261-273 *available at:* DOI: 10.1080/10999922.2005.11051279.

called liberated individual. In this sense, the exercise of liberty becomes a façade as the choices before the individual is in reality is a posed choice.

The PDP Bill, 2019 which envisages the formation of DPAI has various shortcomings one amongst which is the conception of DPAI itself. The bill, though an important landmark in the technological advancement of the country, is not free from its own inconsistencies, which need correction at the behest before the bill transitions into a full-fledged act.

Further, the bill of 2022 is flawed in the sense that it confers excessive powers into the hands of the government and there is much scope for tyrannical usage of the Bill, if it sees the light of the day. The Government needs to revise its framework(s) in light of the needs of India and its diversity. The Government can further not lose sight of the fact of literacy among the individuals and its impact on the glorified use of internet and digital media.

Publisher: Eliva Press Global Ltd

Email: info@elivapress.com

Made in United States
Orlando, FL
04 November 2026

90209890R00024